Tales of the American West

On the
TRAPPING TRAIL

Written by Neil and Ting Morris
Illustrated by Anna Clarke
Historical advisor: Marion Wood

DERRYDALE BOOKS

New York

Published by Evans Brothers Limited
2A Portman Mansions, Chiltern Street
London W1M 1LE

First Published 1988

This 1989 edition published by Derrydale Books, distributed by Crown
Publishers, Inc., 225 Park Avenue South, New York, New York 10003

Printed in Hong Kong by Wing King Tong Co. Ltd.

h g f e d c b a

ISBN 0 517 68024 6

INTRODUCTION

A new nation was born in 1783 when the Revolutionary War ended and the United States gained independence. At that time, the western boundary was formed by the Mississippi River. Beyond was a vast wilderness, the home of wild animals and nomadic tribes of Plains Indians.

In 1803, the United States made the Louisiana Purchase, buying over 1,250,000 square miles of land from the French. For an agreed sum of $15,000,000, this deal more than doubled the territory of the previous 17 states of the young republic. The new land stretched westward from the Mississippi to the Rocky Mountains. Soon, daring pioneers and fur trappers started forging trails into the forests, mountains, and deserts of this unmapped new territory.

When Texas joined the United States, cowboys began driving huge herds of longhorn cattle north. The age of Wild West towns had arrived, and with it, the rush for gold in California. This is the image of the West that has lived on for over a hundred years, kept alive by legends and Hollywood westerns. Between 1810 and 1840, the great fur trade boom attracted many to become trappers. In their search for beaver streams, they became the courageous explorers who opened the land to the pioneers and settlers. Their enemies were wild animals, hostile Indians, and ruthless rivals. Each year in early summer, the trappers met to sell their furs and stock up with fresh supplies.

This story is about one trapper and his son, and their adventures in the wild. The information pages with the rifle border will tell you more about the life and work of the trappers of the Old West.

As the boat went up river, Jake watched his hometown slowly disappear. He was the only youngster among the fur trappers, but he had learned a lot from his father's hunting stories. Jake had always known that one day he would go with him on the trapping trail.

4

When his mother died, Jake had told his father that he was old enough to go with him. "It's hard and dangerous," Joe warned his son. Joe was one of the best beaver trappers in the West, and he usually worked on his own. But he knew Jake would be a companion he could trust.

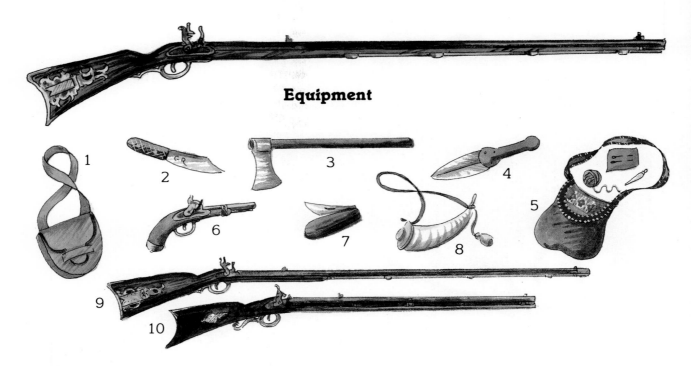

Equipment

Trappers were also called mountain men, because they set their traps in the rivers and streams of the Rocky Mountains. Theirs was a lonely, dangerous life. They admired Indian skills and copied many of their ways. Equipment: 1. Bullet pouch; 2. Green River knife; 3. Axe; 4. Dagger; 5. Possibles bag containing needles, awl, and twine; 6. Percussion cap pistol; 7. Folding knife; 8. Powder horn; 9. Kentucky rifle; 10. Double-barreled Plains rifle.

A. Trappers lit fires by hitting flint with a striker; the sparks caught the punk—the rotten wood which trappers used as tinder.

B. Bullets were made of lead. Molten lead was poured into a metal mold, which opened to give round bullets which were carried in the trappers' bullet pouch.

As they moved upstream, the land grew more wild. Suddenly, they saw smoke signals. "We are in Crow country," Joe told his son. "But we needn't fear the Indians. The Crow chief is my friend." They moved on into the hills.

At the Crow camp, Chief Hawkface made the travelers welcome.
He was happy to trade two of his horses for knives and mirrors.

Little Wolf, the chief's son, showed Jake the Indian way of
hunting. Before leaving, Jake gave him one of his best knives, and
Little Wolf made a gift of his bow and arrow. Now, they were
brothers.

Joe led them over mountains that no man had ever crossed. One evening as they were looking for a good place to camp, a cub joined them. Jake wanted to pick it up, but he felt his father's hand stopping him.

Seconds later, a puma sprang from nowhere, picked up her cub, and was gone. When Jake looked at his father, his finger was still on the trigger.

Their journey took them many weeks. Following the creeks and streams, they at last found beaver dams and lodges. They set their traps and waited. Joe knew from experience that this would be a good place to trap.

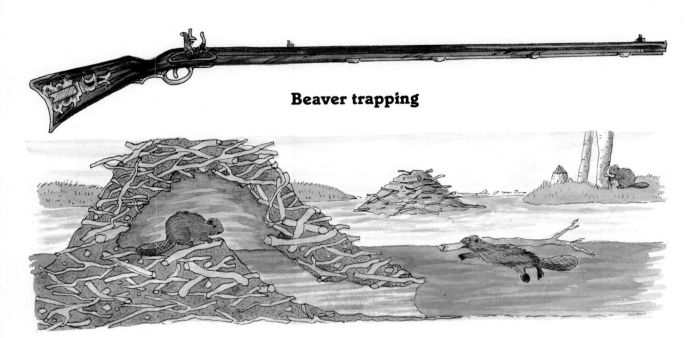

Beaver trapping

Beavers live on land and in water. Using their chisel-like teeth, they cut down trees both for food and to build dams and lodges. They live in the lodge, which they make out of branches and stones pasted together with mud. The entrance is below water so that other animals cannot get inside, but the lodge itself is quite dry.

Trappers caught beavers in the steel traps chained to stakes under water. When the beaver was caught in the trap, it drowned. The beaver skins were stretched on willow frame hoops, pressed, and sold in packs to fur traders. In the 19th century, beaver fur was very fashionable for hats and trimmings.

Every day, they made an excellent catch. There were so many good trapping streams that they decided to build their winter cabin here. Jake soon became an expert bowman.

They took turns hunting for food. One day, Joe said, "I've seen moose tracks in the forest. Tonight we'll have a feast!"

Housing and hunting

Trappers often made winter camp in a log hut or cabin. Or they would live in a tent made of skins on a frame of wooden poles, with a smoke hole at the top. They carried as little as possible except for their blankets, but usually took salt and flour with them.

bobcat beaver buffalo mink hawk

rabbit moose fox reindeer wolf

Trappers hunted many animals for meat. Beaver, mink, and fox were very popular for their fur.

13

Joe tracked the moose through the forest. Suddenly, he came face to face with a huge grizzly bear. He had no time to use his rifle, but suddenly, there was a noise in the trees. Was it the moose? The grizzly raised itself to its full height and turned. Joe pushed past and ran.

Joe was a good runner, but he had never run as fast before. When he knew he was safe, he turned to look for the grizzly. But it had gone. It was only then that he saw the blood.

Hours later, Jake went in search of his father. He found him exhausted and in pain. It was turning colder and starting to snow.

It took them a long time to make their way back. As they neared
home, Joe sensed danger. "Don't move!" he whispered. Hostile
Blackfoot surrounded their cabin. They could only watch as the
Indians robbed them of their horses and pelts.

Sign language

hello

trade

friend

me

summer

winter

horserider

kill

white man

Crow

Apache

Blackfoot

Indian tribes spoke different languages, so they used sign language to communicate with each other. These hand signals were learned by the trappers and explorers who first met and traded with the Indians. Between each sign, the speaker returns his hands to his side to show it is finished.

Joe's wounds healed quickly, and they were soon trapping again. Before long, they had made up for all the stolen pelts.

When the spring thaw came, they made a canoe to carry their pelts. They would soon be going to sell them at the great meeting.

It was hard going. Each time they came to strong rapids or a waterfall, they unloaded the canoe and carried it. It took weeks to reach the great meeting place.

Trading posts

Trappers often used a fort as their base. Here, they sold their furs and stocked up with fresh supplies. Indians who traded their furs camped outside the fort. Fort Laramie was one of the most important trading posts in the Rocky Mountains, and it was later taken over by the American Fur Company.

A great meeting—or "rendezvous"—was held every year in late spring in an agreed place. In addition to being an opportunity for trading, it was a very festive occasion. There was bartering, wrestling and shooting matches, singing and dancing. Many trappers spent most of the money they got for their furs drinking and gambling.

Jake and his father had been by themselves for almost a year. After all this time, it would be good to meet friends again.

Jake spent some time with Little Wolf while his father sold their furs. "When we've sold everything," Joe said to his son, "you must make your decision."

Jake had decided about his future long before now. They got a good price for their furs and bought new traps and equipment. As the days passed, Jake longed to return to the great mountains to find new trapping trails.

This map of the Old West shows the rivers and streams where the mountain men hunted and trapped.

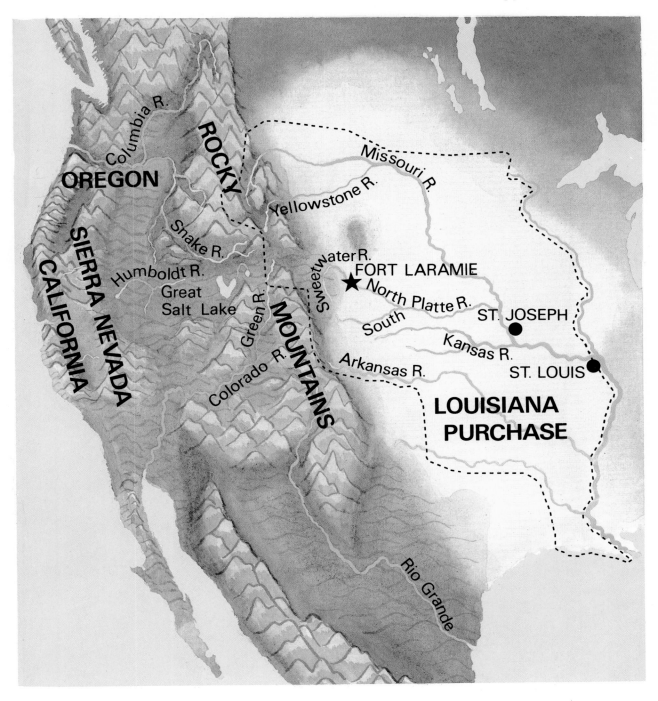

OREGON

ROCKY

Columbia R.

Yellowstone R.

Missouri R.

Snake R.

SIERRA NEVADA

CALIFORNIA

Humboldt R.

Great
Salt Lake

Green R.

Sweetwater R.

MOUNTAINS

FORT LARAMIE

North Platte R.

South

ST. JOSEPH

Kansas R.

Colorado R.

Arkansas R.

ST. LOUIS

LOUISIANA
PURCHASE

Rio Grande

Tales of the American West

LONGHORN
on the Move

Written by Neil and Ting Morris
Illustrated by Anna Clarke
Historical advisor: Marion Wood

DERRYDALE BOOKS

New York

INTRODUCTION

A new nation was born in 1783 when the Revolutionary War ended and the United States gained independence. At that time, the western boundary was formed by the Mississippi River. Beyond was a vast wilderness, the home of wild animals and nomadic tribes of Plains Indians.

In 1803, the United States made the Louisiana Purchase, buying over 1,250,000 square miles of land from the French. For an agreed sum of $15,000,000, this deal more than doubled the territory of the previous 17 states of the young republic. The new land stretched westward from the Mississippi to the Rocky Mountains. Soon, daring pioneers and fur trappers started forging trails into the forests, mountains, and deserts of this unmapped new territory.

When Texas joined the United States, cowboys began driving huge herds of longhorn cattle north. The age of Wild West towns had arrived, and with it, the rush for gold in California. This is the image of the Old West that has lived on for over a hundred years, kept alive by legends and Hollywood westerns.

The cowboys' story began when the Spanish first landed on the shores of Mexico, bringing with them a herd of cattle. Mexican herdsmen later taught their skills to the first Texas cowboys, and the cattle grew strong and healthy on the plains of Texas. When the Civil War ended in 1865, there was a great need for beef in the northern cities. And so began the long cattle drives to Kansas market towns such as Abilene and Dodge City.

This is the story of one young cowboy and his adventures on the long journey north. The information pages with the rifle border will tell you more about the life and work of the cowboys of the Old West.

When Sam reached the ranch, he followed his nose. There was a smell of stew, and he couldn't remember when he'd last had a hot meal. "The name's Sam White," the boy said. "Where's the boss? I'm looking to sign on." The cook knew the boy didn't stand a chance with Marshall, the new trail boss.

"We can't use kids on this drive. Get back to school," Marshall told
Sam. "When I could draw a horse and mark brands on my slate,
I knew I was too smart for school," Sam replied. "All right, let's
see how good you are," Marshall snapped.

Sam had trouble getting on the bucking bronco, but he gripped
tight with his legs and rolled with the horse. "The kid can stay with
me," Maclean said to Marshall.

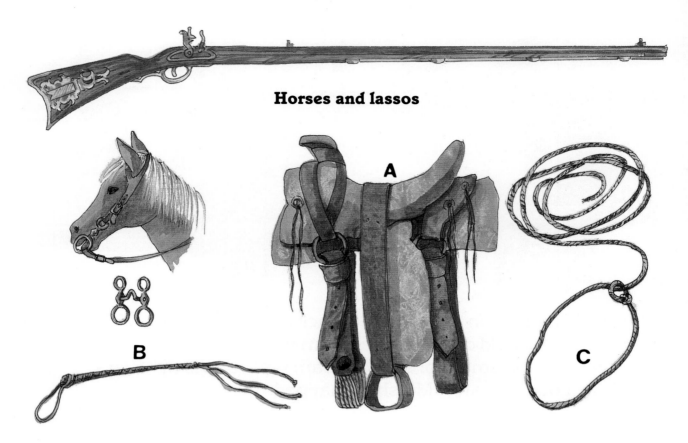

Horses and lassos

Mustangs were wild ponies that had to be caught and tamed before they could be put to work. Bronco busters had the job of breaking them in. Cowboys changed horses several times a day. The horse wrangler looked after the full herd of horses, which was called a remuda.

A. The saddle—the cowboy's most important possession.

B. Bridle, bit, and whip.
C. Lariat or lasso.

The cowboy roped cattle and horses with his lasso or lariat, which hung loosely coiled from his saddle horn. To rope animals, the cowboy built a loop, whirled it in the air to keep it open, and tossed it over the animal's head. He wrapped his end of the rope around his saddle horn. In addition to roping animals, the lasso was used to build corrals, pull wagons, haul firewood, and hang cattle thieves.

Sam was up early next morning, ready to help with the roundup. But Marshall had already left. When Sam rode out, he saw a wisp of smoke and men with branding irons. One of them waved his hat. Sam knew this was a warning to stay away. Suddenly, Sam recognized the rustler's face. It was Marshall.

"I must warn them back at the ranch," Sam thought as he turned his horse. But who would believe a runaway kid? He would probably never make it anyway, with the rustlers after him. At that moment, two riders appeared in the distance.

Shots rang out, and Marshall and his men sped off. Sam was ready to go after them, but Maclean stopped him. "Don't bother with that thief," he said. "I'll make sure he never heads a drive again."

Branding longhorn

The Texas longhorn; long-legged and tough; average horn spread 4 to 5 feet; average weight 850 pounds.

Cattle first came to America from Spain. They were left to run loose over the plains of Mexico, California, and Texas and developed into the Texas longhorn, the great cattle herd of the Old West. After the Civil War, they were rounded up and driven north, where there was a great demand for beef. Their horns took many different shapes.

Each rancher had his own brand that marked his cattle. Because there were no fences, herds wandered for miles, and stray calves had to be branded and earmarked. Rustlers were cattle thieves, ruthless cowboys who took unbranded calves and put their own brand on them. They also stole older, branded cattle and changed the owner's brand with a cinch ring or a running iron. This was known as brand blotting.

1. Branding iron; 2. Cinch ring; 3. Running iron.

Sam was treated like a regular cowhand. Maclean was the new trail boss, and he put Sam in charge of the horses. On the first day, the men drove the cattle as far as they could. Longhorn never liked leaving their home range.

Sam and the horses stayed with the wagon. Cook made a hot stew, and at sundown, the riders started coming in. But it was hours before the longhorn settled down. Then, at last, the cowboys could rest for the night.

Cowboy's equipment

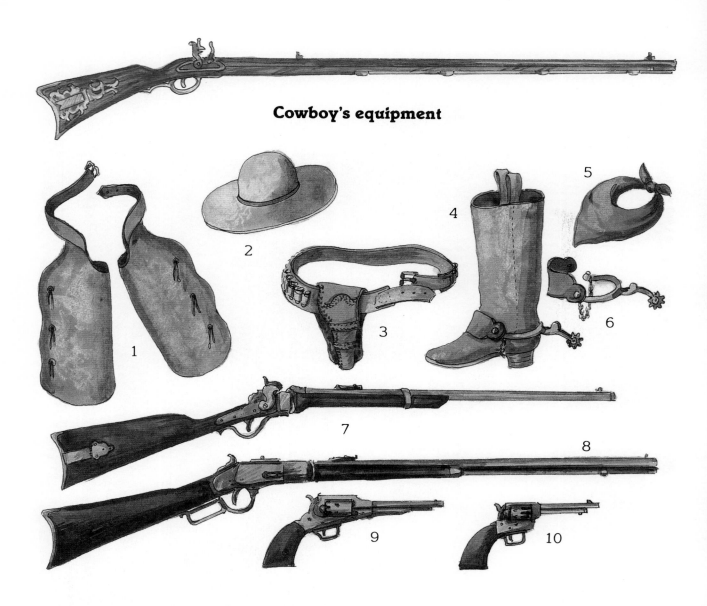

1. Chaps, to protect his legs against scratches, rope burns, and horns;
2. Stetson; 3. Belt and holster; 4. Boots, with high heels to stop feet from slipping through stirrups; 5. Neckerchief, to protect the neck from the sun; in a dust storm, it was worn over the nose and mouth; 6. Spurs, to make the horse speed up; 7. Sharps rifle; 8. Winchester rifle; 9. Remington revolver; 10. Colt "Peacemaker".

Day after day, they traveled endless miles across the dry, barren land. There was little noise, as the ground seemed to swallow the trampling of the hooves. But the cattle were getting edgy. They needed water.

Then, for the first time for days, the cattle sensed they were near water. Suddenly, the lead steer broke into a run. The cowboys rode hard to keep the cattle from going crazy. Sam caught up with the steer just in time to pull him out of the quicksand.

"It's a poison lake!" Maclean yelled, as the cattle followed their
leader toward the quicksand and the pool. The cowboys fought
to keep the maddened animals away from the poisoned water.
But, for some, it was too late.

As they reached a river at last, the sky darkened. The cowboys feared a stampede. Lightning could sometimes set a whole herd off. They let the cattle drink as much as they could take.

But the cattle didn't want to cross the fast-flowing river. "Show them the way," Maclean shouted to Sam. At once, he drove the horses in front of the longhorn.

The cattle followed the horses across the torrent. But they were scared, and half-way across, they started milling around. There was chaotic shouting as the cowboys tried to break the jam.

On the trail

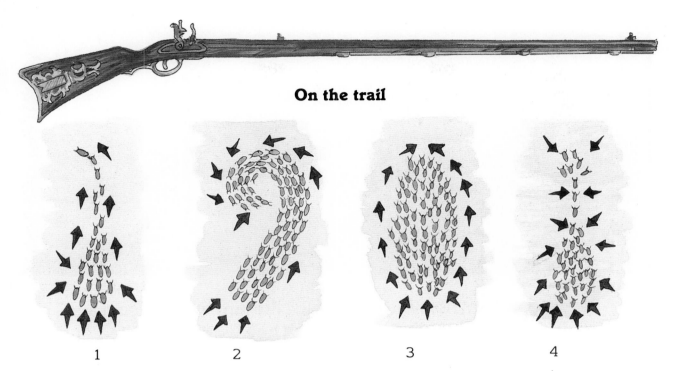

1   2   3   4

These diagrams show how the cowboys controlled a herd on the trail. The arrows are the riders, who took up special positions to make the longhorn do what they wanted them to.

1. Turning the herd to the left.
2. Stopping a stampede; the riders turn the leaders to make the herd mill around in a circle. 3. Holding the herd still.
4. Counting the herd.

The cook was a most important member of the trail outfit. He was in charge of the chuck wagon, which held all the food, cooking utensils, and extra supplies for the drive. It as an ordinary farm wagon with a box bolted on the back. The cook's last job each night was to point the chuck wagon north, so that everyone knew which way to head in the morning.

Sam never found out how the men broke the jam. No one said a word as they gulped down their coffee. They were exhausted. It was Sam's turn on night duty, but Maclean said, "The kid needs rest."

But Sam couldn't sleep. He listened to the night guard's song. Suddenly, there was a shout and the sound of six-shooters. The cattle quickly got to their feet.

The earth trembled beneath the hooves of the thundering herd.
A group of Indian warriors were driving the cattle off. Sam rode
after them with the men, but suddenly, a shot wounded his
horse.

It took them till sunrise to round up the cattle. Then Maclean followed the Indians to their camp. The trail boss demanded to speak to their chief, and he soon found out who was behind the raid.

The Indians returned the stolen cattle and Marshall in exchange for five longhorn. "I should have known it was you," Maclean told Marshall. "I'll see you get locked away at the end of the trail."

The cattle town

The trail ended in a cattle town. From there, the cattle were taken by railroad to cities in the east. Stockyards, cattle pens, and loading chutes were built beside the railroad. Cattle towns became wild places where the cowboys, after months on the trail, drank too much and got very rowdy. The townspeople hired a sheriff to keep law and order.

After three long months of heat and dust, it was good to see the town. Maclean handed Marshall over to the sheriff, and the herd was sold. Sam's pockets were full of money. "You've done a good job," Maclean said to Sam. "Now have a little fun and a lot of sleep. You've earned them both!"

This map of the Old West shows the trails the cowboys used to drive the longhorn north to the cattle towns.

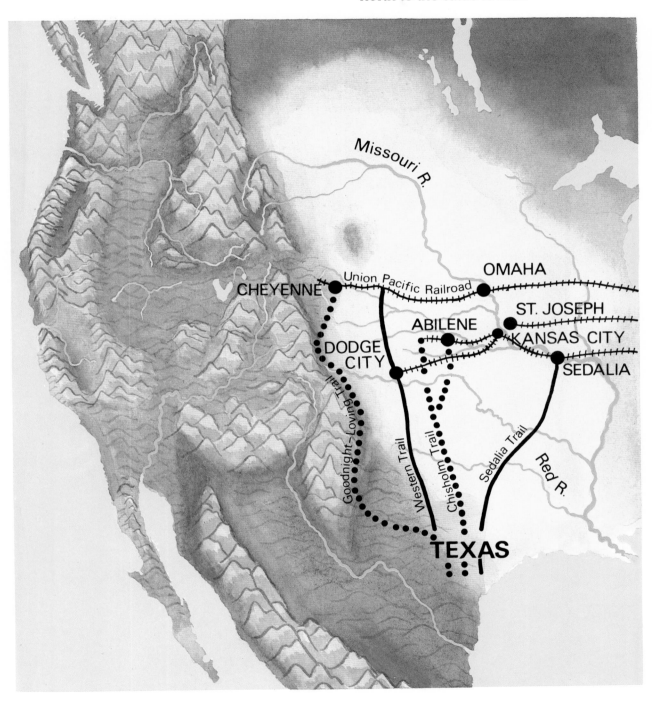

Tales of the American West

WAGON WHEELS
Roll West

Written by Neil and Ting Morris
Illustrated by Anna Clarke
Historical advisor: Marion Wood

DERRYDALE BOOKS

New York

INTRODUCTION

A new nation was born in 1783 when the Revolutionary War ended and the United States gained independence. At that time, the western boundary was formed by the Mississippi River. Beyond was a vast wilderness, the home of wild animals and nomadic tribes of Plains Indians.

In 1803, the United States made the Louisiana Purchase, buying over 1,250,000 square miles of land from the French. For an agreed sum of $15,000,000, this deal more than doubled the territory of the previous 17 states of the young republic. The new land stretched westward from the Mississippi to the Rocky Mountains. Soon, daring pioneers and fur trappers started forging trails into the forests, mountains, and deserts of this unmapped new territory.

After 1840, thousands of families traveled along the Oregon and California trails to the Far West to seek a new life. The early pioneers traveled toward a land that was largely unknown, with no maps or journals to guide them. Families of pioneers joined together for safety, but the wagon trains faced a difficult, dangerous journey. Not everyone made it to their intended new home.

This is the story of one pioneer family, and their adventures on the long journey west. The information pages with the rifle border will tell you more about the life and work of the pioneers of the Old West.

The long line of wagons moved slowly through the wilderness.
When they reached the river, the oxen plunged in, and the wagon
wheels rumbled over the stony bottom. Anna was walking next
to her father when the wagon jolted to a halt. He pushed hard, but
the wagon would not move.

"Another broken axle," Anna's father said. "Take Beth and the boys and follow the others," said her mother. "We'll soon catch up with you." "I want my spade," Bob cried. He never went anywhere without it, just in case he came across gold.

"Don't cry, Beth," Anna said gently, "we are going to the promised land." That is what their father had told them when they set off on the trail to Oregon. There, they would have their own farm, but it was such a long journey.

The wagon

feed trough

toolbox

brake lever   tar pot   water keg

The wagon was a home on wheels, a hospital, and a fortress. Oxen pulled the wagons, which carried the family's furniture, food supplies, cooking utensils, and other essential belongings.

Families of pioneers joined together for safety and traveled in groups of at least ten wagons. The wagon train set off in spring from outfitting towns like Independence and St. Joseph in Missouri. The journey took about five months. The travelers elected a wagon master, and mountain men acted as scouts and guides. The first settlers traveled to Oregon in 1839, and to California a year later.

With the new axle, there were no more breakdowns. It was Jim's turn to steer the wagon, as Father looked through the spyglass. "Can you see the others?" Jim shouted. He too had seen a huge cloud of dust.

There was no time to explain. A herd of buffalo was charging straight toward them. Father cracked his whip, and Jim drove the wagon hard. They had to get out of the way fast!

When they had caught up with the others, Anna saw how lucky they had been. Some had lost all their belongings. Anna felt proud of her father. They would always be safe with him. The boys were enjoying the freshly cooked buffalo meat, but Anna kept thinking of the huge brown animals thundering past.

On the move

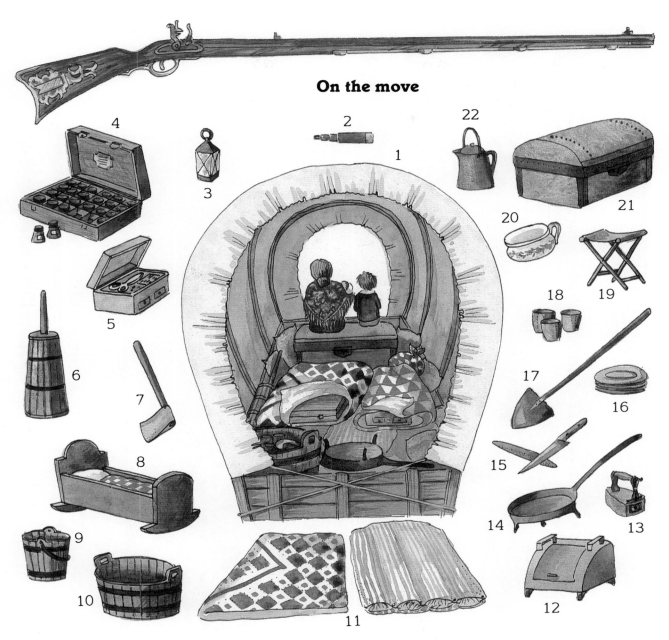

The pioneers took clothes, blankets, tents, and spare parts for the wagon. They made sure they had enough food to last five to six months. On the plains, they killed buffalo for fresh meat. They also took cattle to provide meat and milk.

1. Wagon; 2. Spyglass; 3. Lantern; 4. Medicine box; 5. Sewing box; 6. Butterchurn; 7. Axe; 8. Cradle; 9. Bucket; 10. Washtub; 11. Quilt and mattress; 12. Reflector oven; 13. Iron; 14. Skillet; 15. Whetstone and knife; 16. Pewter plates; 17. Spade; 18. Patent leather cups; 19. Camp stool; 20. Chamber pot; 21. Trunk; 22. Coffee pot.

They pressed on to reach the fort before nightfall. "You'll never get those wagons over the mountains," the trappers warned them. "Indian tribes are on the war path, defending their hunting grounds." Anna watched the Indian girl and her child. Why couldn't they be friends, she wondered.

It had not rained for days, and as they climbed, they got further and further away from the river. The children were thirsty, but they said nothing. They knew that the last waterskin must be kept for baby Beth.

That night, Anna heard her father tell her mother that he could not go on guard duty. His face was as white as chalk. "You'll feel better in the morning," Mother said. "I'll look after things."

Defending the wagon train

Wagon trains needed to be constantly on the watch for bands of hostile Indians. Lone wagons were an easy target for Indian war parties. At night the wagons were formed into a circle, which served as a corral for the animals and a fortress against attack.

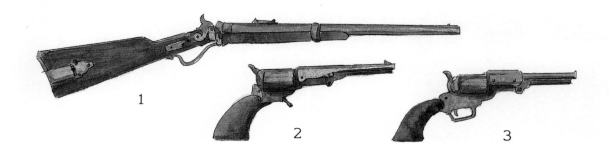

If Indians attacked, the pioneers defended themselves from behind the barrier of wagons. Although at first the Indians were armed only with bows and arrows, lances and tomahawks, they could shoot eight arrows in the time it took to load the pioneers' rifles.
1. Sharps carbine; 2. Paterson Colt;
3. Walker Colt

But next morning, Father was worse, and they could not move on. "I'll find gold," Bob said. "Then we can buy medicine for Father." Anna did not have the heart to remind her little brother that there were no stores in the wilderness.

Jim brought some cactus leaves. "They taste sweet and juicy," he said. The children were all chewing when their mother came out of the wagon. She did not have to say anything—they knew at once. Father was dead.

They had to catch up with the other wagons. Mother placed a cross where they buried father. "Now, he'll never see the promised land," Anna thought, and felt drops on her cheeks. "Rain!" Jim shouted. They had not said a word since Father died. Bob licked the rain. "We'll be all right," Mother said.

A terrible storm raged all night. Outside, their frightened animals panted in terror. Suddenly, they heard the howl of a wolf. It came from beneath the wagon. There was a rustling sound. "It's coming in!" Bob screamed.

"Don't shoot!" Jim cried. "It's a boy!" The Indian child looked terrified, but he was glad for the shelter the family offered. When the storm stopped, he took off his moccasins and gave them to Jim. Then, he left as suddenly as he had appeared.

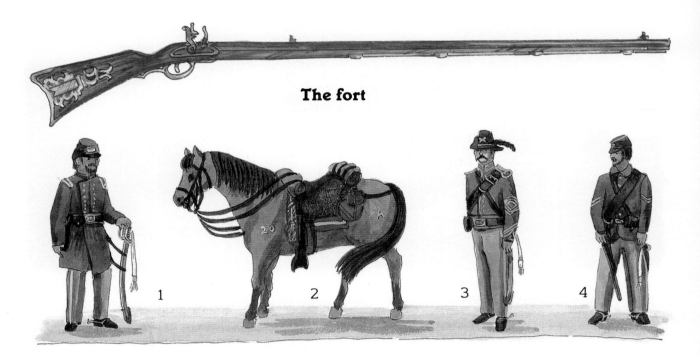

The fort

1   2   3   4

The United States Cavalry (soldiers on horseback) helped to keep law and order in the Old West and fought in the wars against the Indians. They were armed with sabers, revolvers, and carbines.

1. Major, Third Cavalry; 2. Cavalry horse;
3. Sergeant Major, Second Dragoons;
4. Corporal, Second Dragoons.

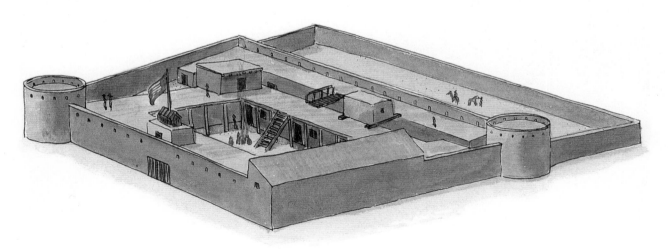

The Cavalry was stationed in forts such as Fort Laramie. In addition to being military stations, the forts were used as trading posts. They were also resting points and supply stations for pioneer wagon trains heading west.

The journey was much easier now. Jim wore his Indian
moccasins all the time. When they saw smoke rising behind the
hill, Bob said: "Why can't we go to that Indian village? I want
moccasins, too. My shoes are all torn." Mother promised to make
moccasins for all of them.

She did not tell the children that she could no longer make out any trail, and there was no trace of the other wagons. All she thought of was getting across the icy streams before snow blocked the passes. Already, the nights were freezing.

By now, they had lost their cattle and made the wagon into a cart. Whenever they climbed one mountain ridge, there was another one ahead. But this time they could not believe what they saw— gold prospectors.

The goldrush

In 1848, gold was discovered at a sawmill in California, and when the news got out, people were gripped by "gold fever." The big rush started in the spring of 1849, but many of the "Forty-Niners," as these gold-seekers became known, did not strike it rich. One man in every five died. Gold camps soon dotted the West. Prospectors panned the rivers and mined the hills for gold-rich pebbles.

Miners sifted the sand from the riverbed with metal pans. Heavy gold dust settled at the bottom.

Rockers were used to separate gold from the gravel.

In a sluice box, a constant flow of water washed the gravel; the waterwheel sped up this operation.

"There is enough gold for all," the prospectors said. But the children knew that their mother would not join the gold-diggers. They were bound for Oregon and the farm. While they mended their wagon and clothes, Bob went off with his spade to dig for gold.

"Why couldn't we stay with them?" Bob cried.
"We wouldn't have found gold anyway," his mother consoled him.
"I found some," the boy said and pulled out a gold nugget.

The boys and baby Beth always fell asleep as soon as they were tucked in, but Anna tried to stay awake. She hated the howl of the wolves, and Mother never dared put the rifle down. They all missed Father terribly.

They kept going day after day, through snow and ice, climbing ridge after mountain ridge. Then, suddenly, they reached the last one. Far below them lay a green valley. "Oregon," Mother said, "where we will have our own farm." Together they walked down the last slope into their new life.

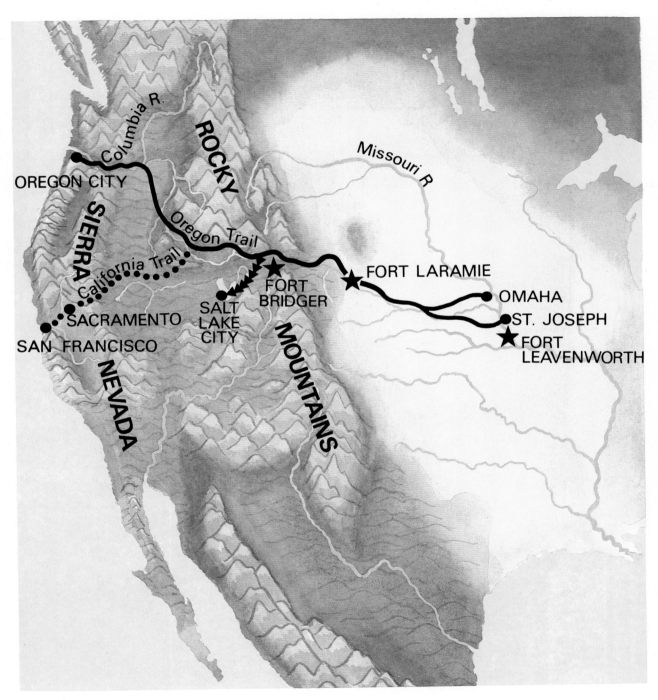

This map of the American West shows the trails traveled by the pioneers across the Western plains to reach Oregon, California, and Salt Lake City.

Tales of the American West

Home on
THE PRAIRIE

Written by Neil and Ting Morris
Illustrated by Anna Clarke
Historical advisor: Marion Wood

DERRYDALE BOOKS

New York

INTRODUCTION

A new nation was born in 1783 when the Revolutionary War ended and the United States gained independence. At that time, the western boundary was formed by the Mississippi River. Beyond was a vast wilderness, the home of wild animals and nomadic tribes of Plains Indians.

In 1803, the United States made the Louisiana Purchase, buying over 1,250,000 square miles of land from the French. For an agreed sum of $15,000,000, this deal more than doubled the territory of the previous 17 states of the young republic. The new land stretched westward from the Mississippi to the Rocky Mountains. Soon, daring pioneers and fur trappers started forging trails into the forests, mountains, and deserts of this unmapped new territory.

In 1862, Congress passed the Homestead Act. This law allowed any adult to have 160 acres of land if they put up their own house and produced a crop within five years. The settlers who came west to take up land did not see themselves as taking territory from the native Indians: they came to find good farming land. At first, the settlers used sod or turf as building materials, but when they could afford or find the wood, they built more substantial log cabins. The new railroads opened up the West and attracted even more people to settle on the prairies.

This is the story of one family of settlers and their adventures on the prairie. The information pages with the rifle border will tell you more about the life and work of the settlers of the Old West.

After weeks of traveling, Father stopped the wagon. "This is our new home," he said. "But where is the house?" the girls asked. "We'll build it right here," Father told them. "Why not closer to the river?" asked Tom. "Because this is Indian country, and we don't want enemies," his mother said.

The girls quickly felt at home. "Look at the flowers we picked for you," Rosy said when her mother came back with water. "There's no one at the creek," she told her husband. But Tom had found Indian tracks. "Can't be too careful," he said. "*I'll* go for water from now on."

Homes

There were few trees on the prairie, so the settlers used sod or turf as building material. Blocks of sod were built up like a brick wall. Door and window frames were made from packing cases. Cracks were filled in with mud.

Some homesteaders made their homes in dugouts. They dug a cave into the side of a hill so that they only needed to build a front wall.

Shanties were made of rough boards and had tar paper roofs. They were hot in summer and drafty in winter. Settlers piled earth against the outside walls to keep warm.

As soon as the family could afford the wood, they built a log cabin with a wooden floor. The settlers' houses had no plumbing, and the privy was in an outhouse.

Soon, they planted their first crops. But one day, when they were plowing, their last blade broke. "I've talked it over with your mother," Father said. "We're out of money. I'll get a job on the railroad and be back in time for harvest."

Tom begged his father to let him come. "Two of us stand a better chance of getting a job," he said. "Mother and the girls will be safe on their own. I've kept a lookout, and there are no new Indian tracks. They've gone for good."

Tom had finally got his way. He and his father were hired as tracklayers, but it was hard and dangerous work. The crew worked in constant danger of attack by Indians. The tribes feared the "iron horse" that was spreading across their land. It was an all-out war for survival.

Railroads

The Central Pacific woodburning locomotive, Jupiter.

In 1862, two companies began work on a railroad between the Missouri River and the Pacific coast. This railroad opened up the Far West and attracted more people to settle on the prairie. The Central Pacific track was built eastward from Sacramento, and the Union Pacific track went west. The two lines followed the California trail and met up in May, 1869.

Building a railroad was hard work. Chinese coolies laid most of the tracks for the Central Pacific. To blast a way through the sides of the mountains, men were lowered in baskets. For blasting, black gunpowder was fired from close up. The men only had handtools, picks, shovels, and saws. Often, the track-laying crew worked in danger of Indian attacks. The native tribes feared that the "iron horse" would bring more buffalo hunters and settlers into their territory.

81

Tom was posted as a lookout, and every day, he saw hundreds of buffalo killed. They provided meat for the railroad workers, but most of the animals were left to rot. There were times when Tom could understand the Indians' anger.

One night, Indian warriors attacked. When they had been beaten off, Tom's father told him he must go home. "There have been massacres all over the plains. You must go and look after your mother and sisters," he said.

Tom knew his father was right. He had never seen so many Indians on the war path. He left at once and took the stagecoach from the nearest stopping place to speed up the journey.

"Not long now," Tom thought. Suddenly, two masked riders appeared. "Throw down the box!" a voice shouted. The driver unchained the strongbox as Tom pulled the trigger. His bullets hit the bandits. "Tie them up and take them to the sheriff," Tom said. "I'll take the horses as my reward!"

Travel in the West

Before the railroads spread across the West, stagecoaches carried passengers, mail, and valuables. One of the most famous stagecoaches was the Concord. It carried up to 14 passengers, with room for their luggage and a strongbox for valuables. Guards, riding "shotgun," usually went along to protect the coach against bandits and Indian attacks. The biggest stagecoach line was run by the Wells Fargo company.

The fastest mail service—13 days from East to West—was run by relays of pony express riders. They used the California trail and changed their ponies three times at relay stations along the route. Pony express riders were boys chosen for their lightness, speed, and fearlessness. The pony express service only lasted 18 months. Once the telegraph lines were opened, messages could travel in Morse code in a few minutes.

Tom rode as fast as he could. But, when he reached the creek near home, he saw a new trail and then . . . teepees . . . many teepees and Indian braves, women, and children. Tom felt really scared. Were his mother and sisters still alive?

He rode on, through the fields where the wheat was now growing high. And there was the little house. He shivered when he saw two Indians leaving. What had they done to his family?

"Mother, thank heavens you are all right," Tom cried.
"We are fine, Tom," his mother said. "The Indians didn't harm us.
They gave us water in exchange for my cornbread and some of
father's tobacco. But now we have run out of everything, and
there is no more water."

Water

The settlers often dug a well near their sod houses or log cabins and hauled water up in buckets.

Sometimes, the water was very deep underground, and farmers built windmills to haul up the water. To find water, a so-called "water witch," or deviner, used a Y-shaped willow switch. When the switch trembled, it meant that water lay directly below.

Where there were rivers, settlers dug ditches and built wooden sluiceways to bring water down to their farms.

Tom promised his mother that from now on they would have
their own water. Early the next day, he started digging a well.
"More rope!" he shouted from the deep pit, and then, "Water!"
"It's the best water I've ever tasted," Rosy said.

They were all so excited that they hardly noticed the terrible heat
that was growing and growing. Suddenly, Tom saw a wall of
flames moving across the open plain towards them.

They were saved by a torrential rain storm. Water came pouring through all the cracks and the roof. "Get under the table," Mother shouted as the roof came crashing down. Luckily, no one was hurt. "We'll build a stronger and better house next time," Tom told his sisters.

"All our work has been destroyed," Tom said to his mother. "The crops Father planted; the house you made our home."
"But we are all well, Tom, and that's what matters most," she said. "It's harvest time, and Father will be back soon."

Tom ran down to the creek. The teepees had gone. The Indians had moved on. He looked around at the trees. "We could build a log cabin," he thought. "This is Indian country." His mother's words came back to him.

"But it's our country, too," Tom thought as he ran back. There was a wagon outside their broken home, loaded with timber. His father was back. "There won't be much harvesting," Father said, "so let's start the house. I brought plenty of wood."
"And there's more by the creek," Tom said.

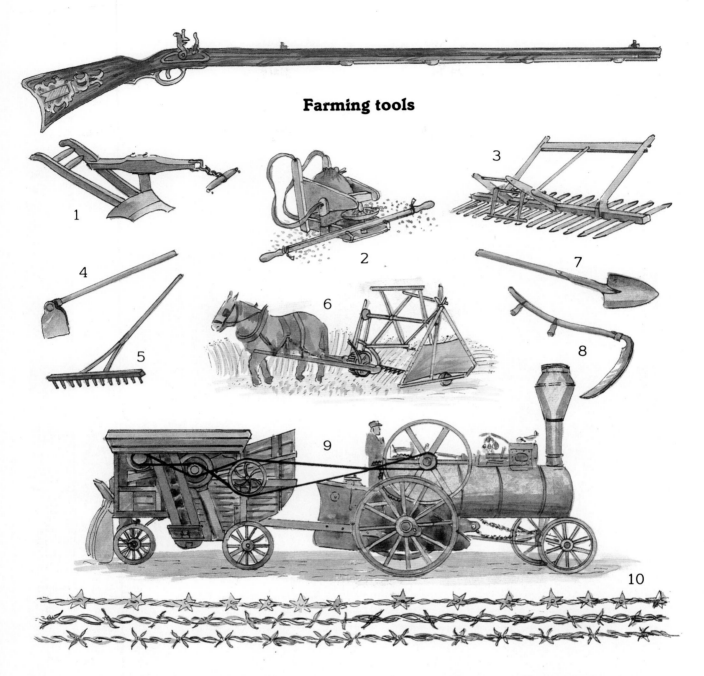

Farming tools

Horses and oxen were used to pull farm machines, and steam engines were introduced later.
1. Plow; 2. Seed fiddle. It was claimed that a sower with a fiddle could sow up to four acres an hour; 3. Hay rake; 4. Hoe; 5. Rake; 6. Reaper; 7. Spade; 8. Scythe; 9. Thresher powered by steam engine; 10. Barbed wire. Its use helped hardworking settlers to farm the land without fear of longhorn cattle trampling their crops.

Within a few days, they moved into the new log cabin. "When will our beds be ready?" the girls asked.
"At bedtime," father said. "And remember, whatever you dream on your first night will come true." For Tom, their dream had already come true—a real home on the prairie.

This map of the Old West shows the railroad and stagecoach routes which the settlers used to travel westward.

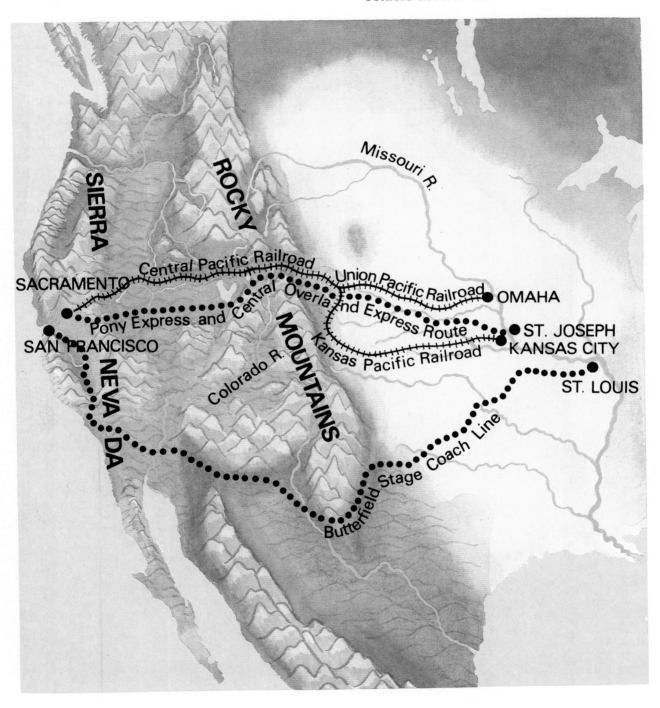

Missouri R.

SIERRA

ROCKY

SACRAMENTO

Central Pacific Railroad

Union Pacific Railroad

OMAHA

Pony Express and Central

Overland Express Route

ST. JOSEPH

SAN FRANCISCO

NEVADA

Kansas Pacific Railroad

KANSAS CITY

MOUNTAINS

Colorado R.

ST. LOUIS

Butterfield Stage Coach Line